psychedelic stress-relieving
sea creatures

This is a work of fiction. All sea creatures depicted as engaging in psychedelic activity are at least eighteen years old. This book contains ready-to-color pages.

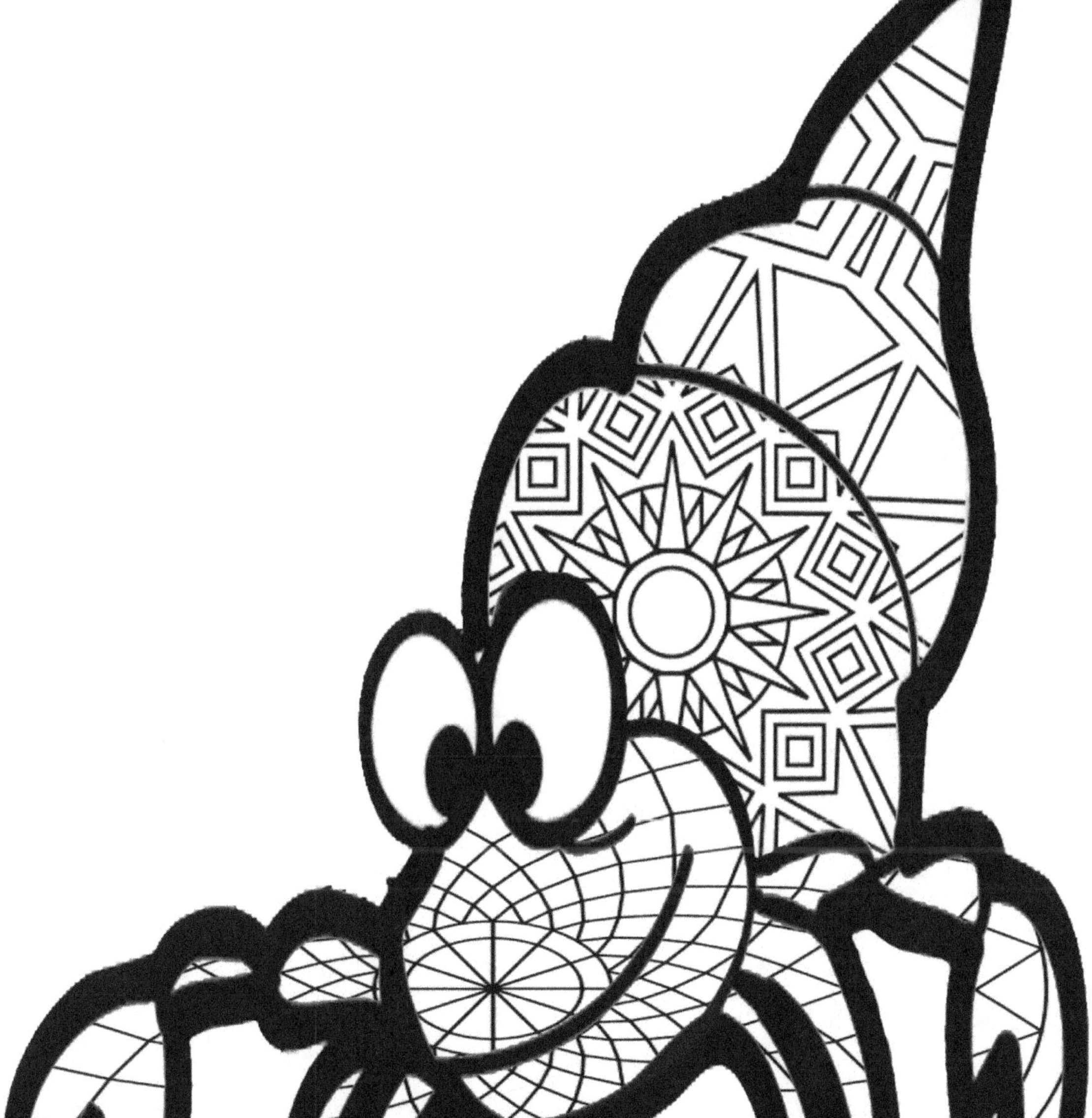

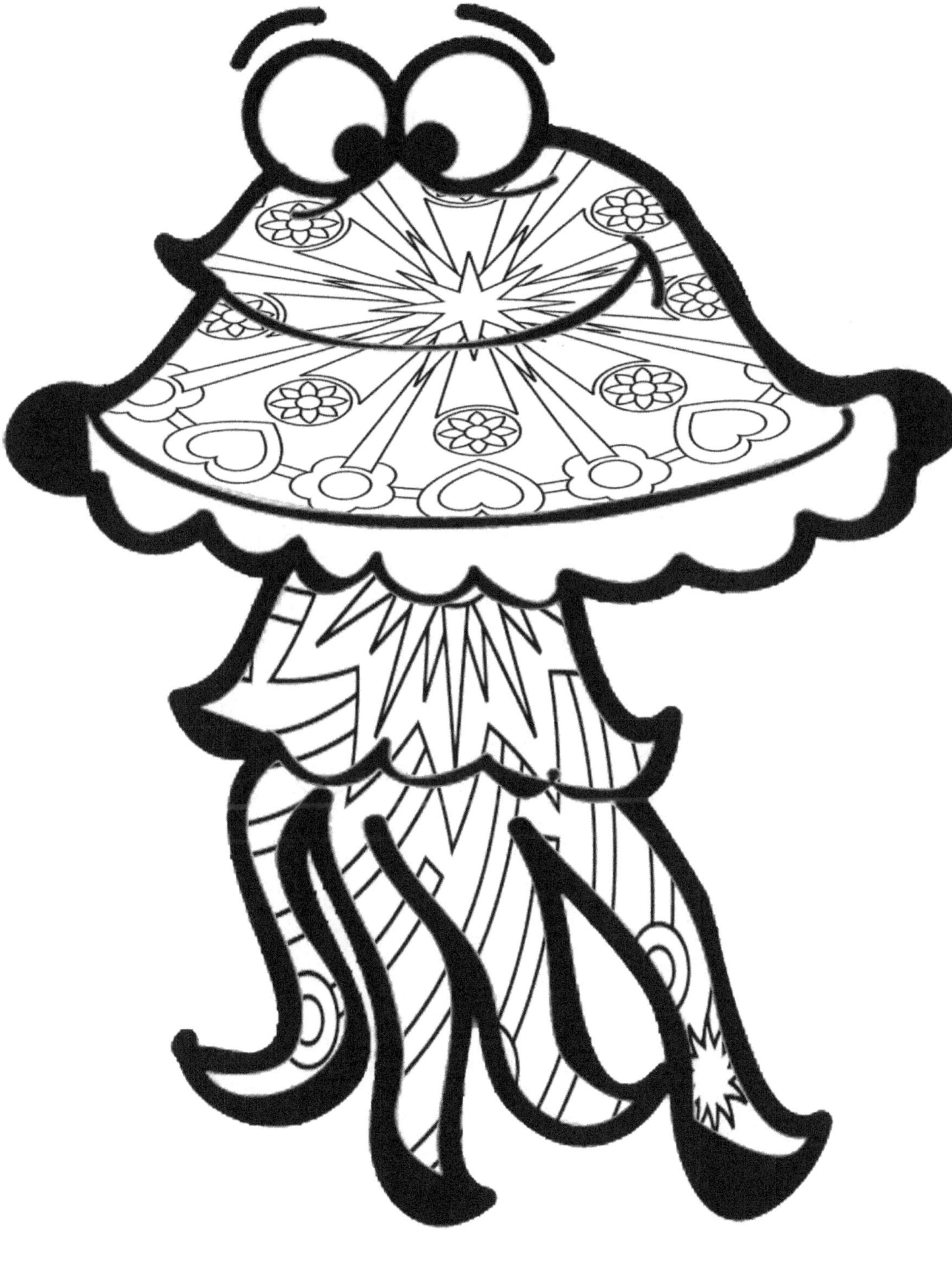

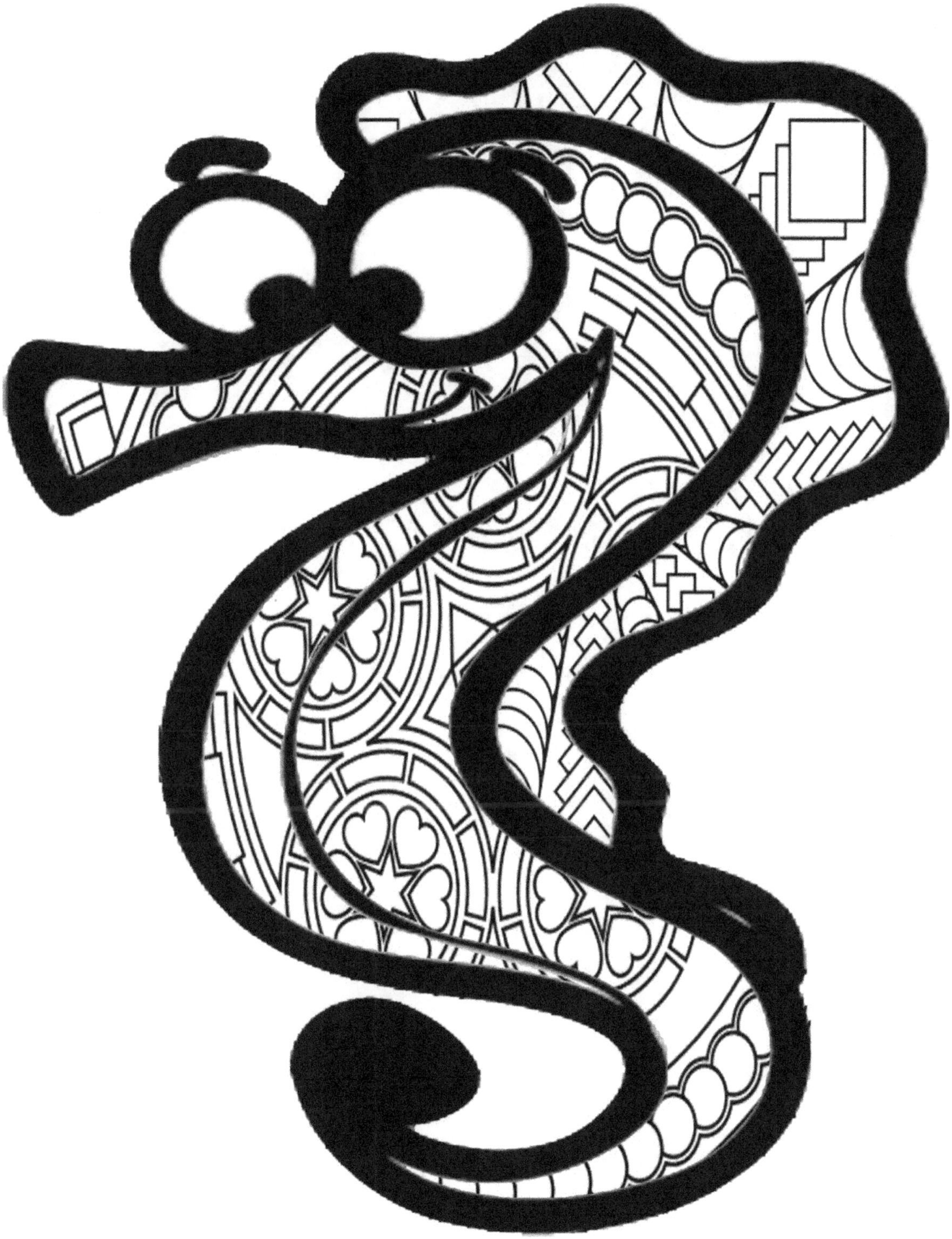

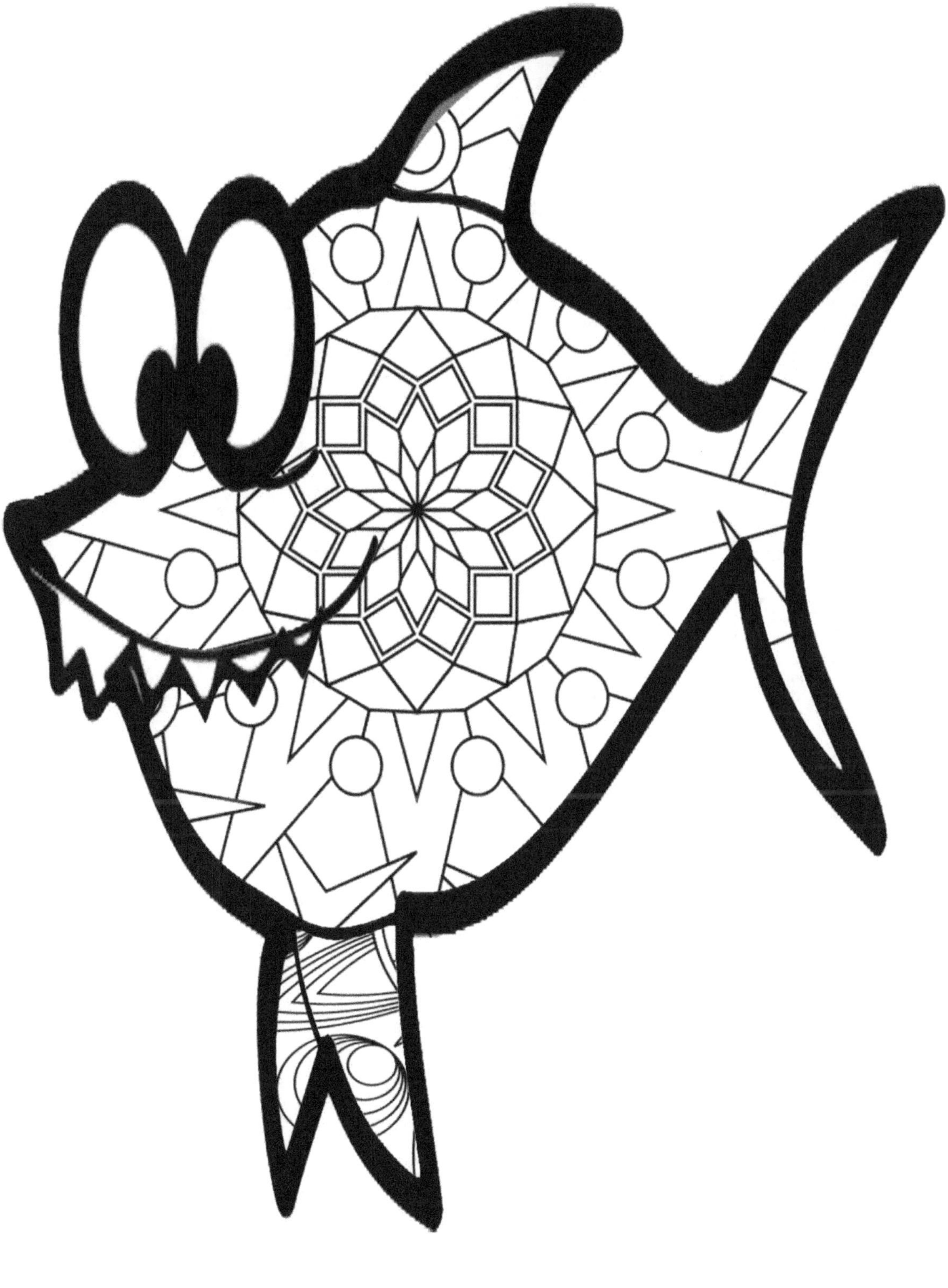

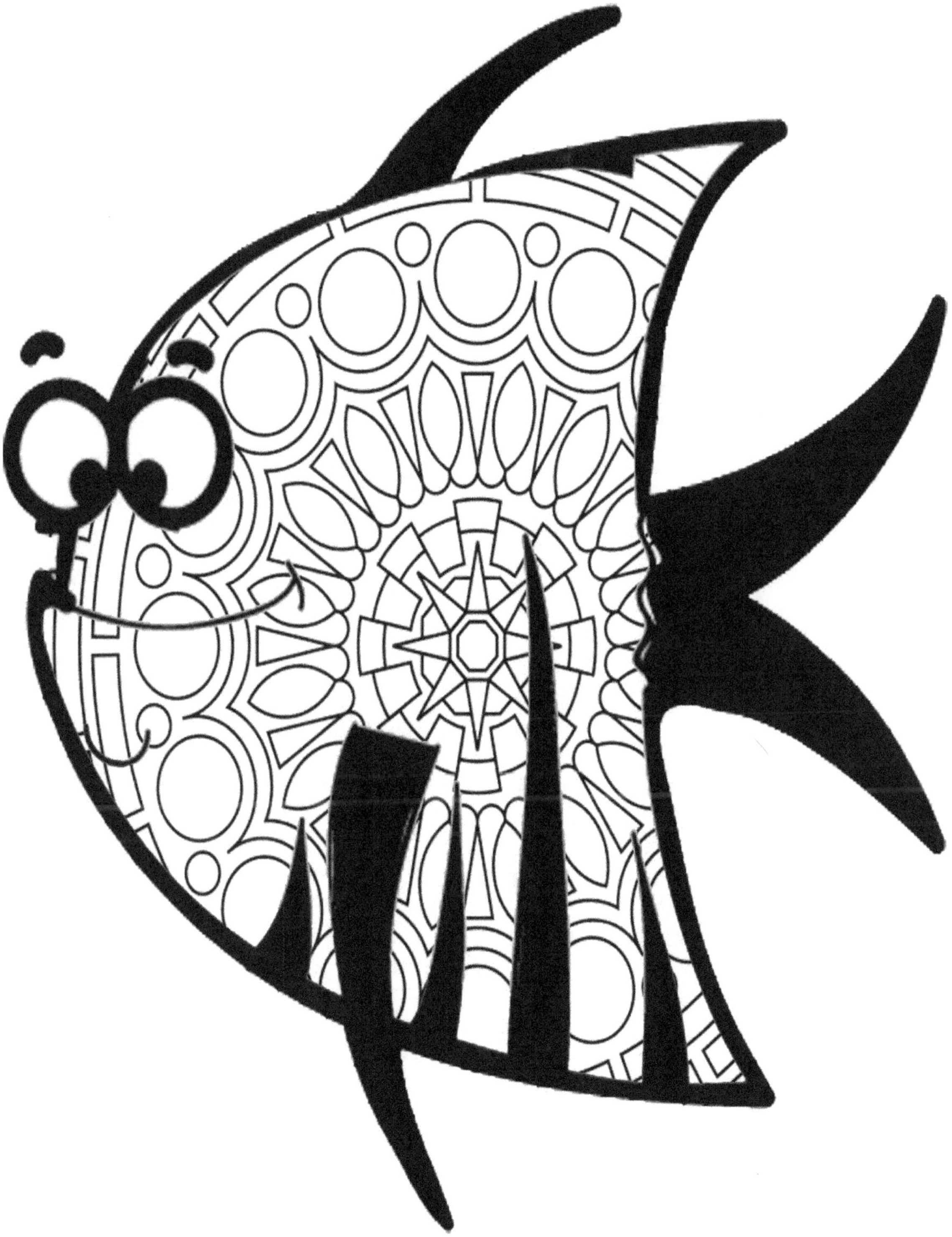

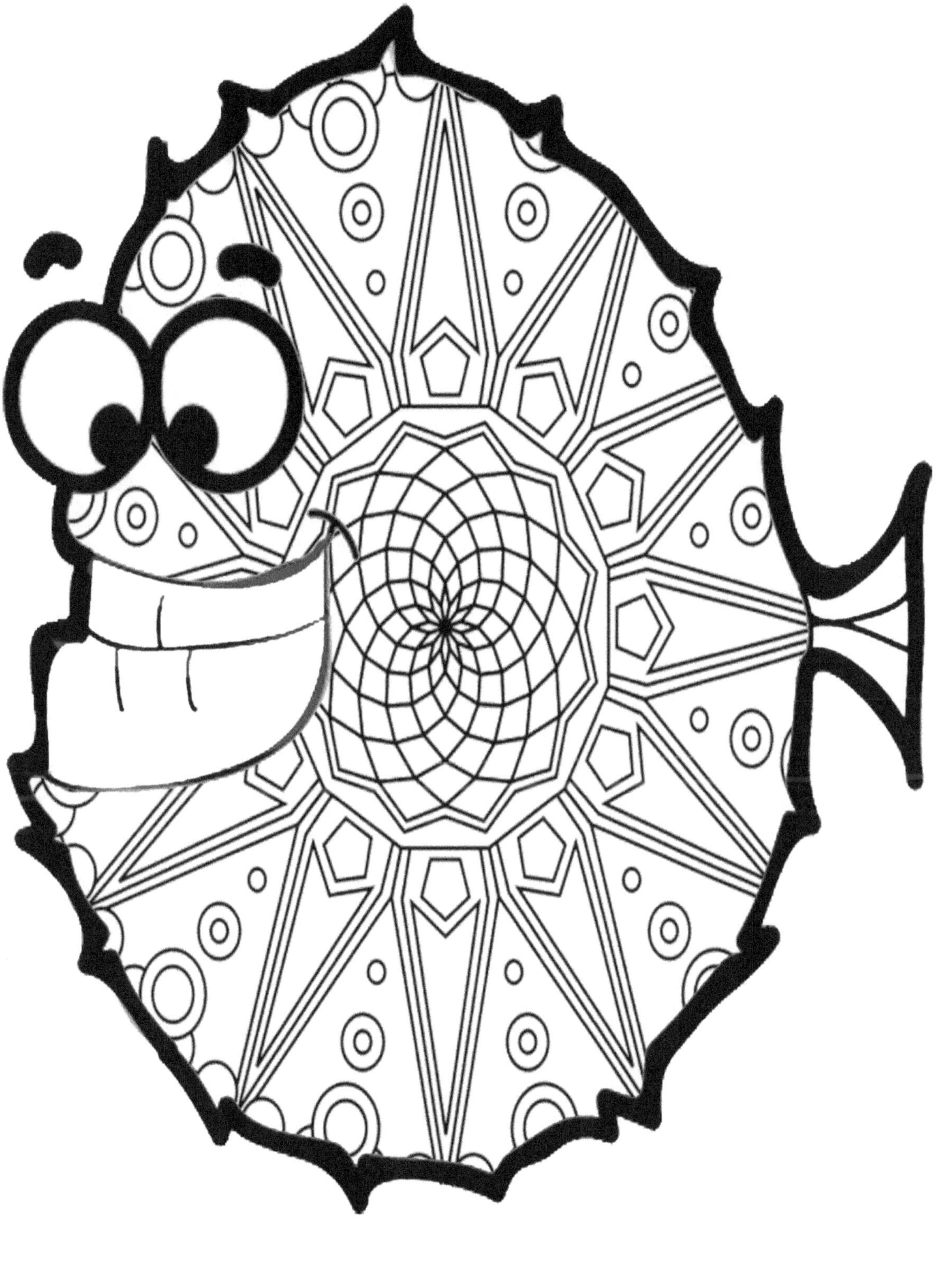

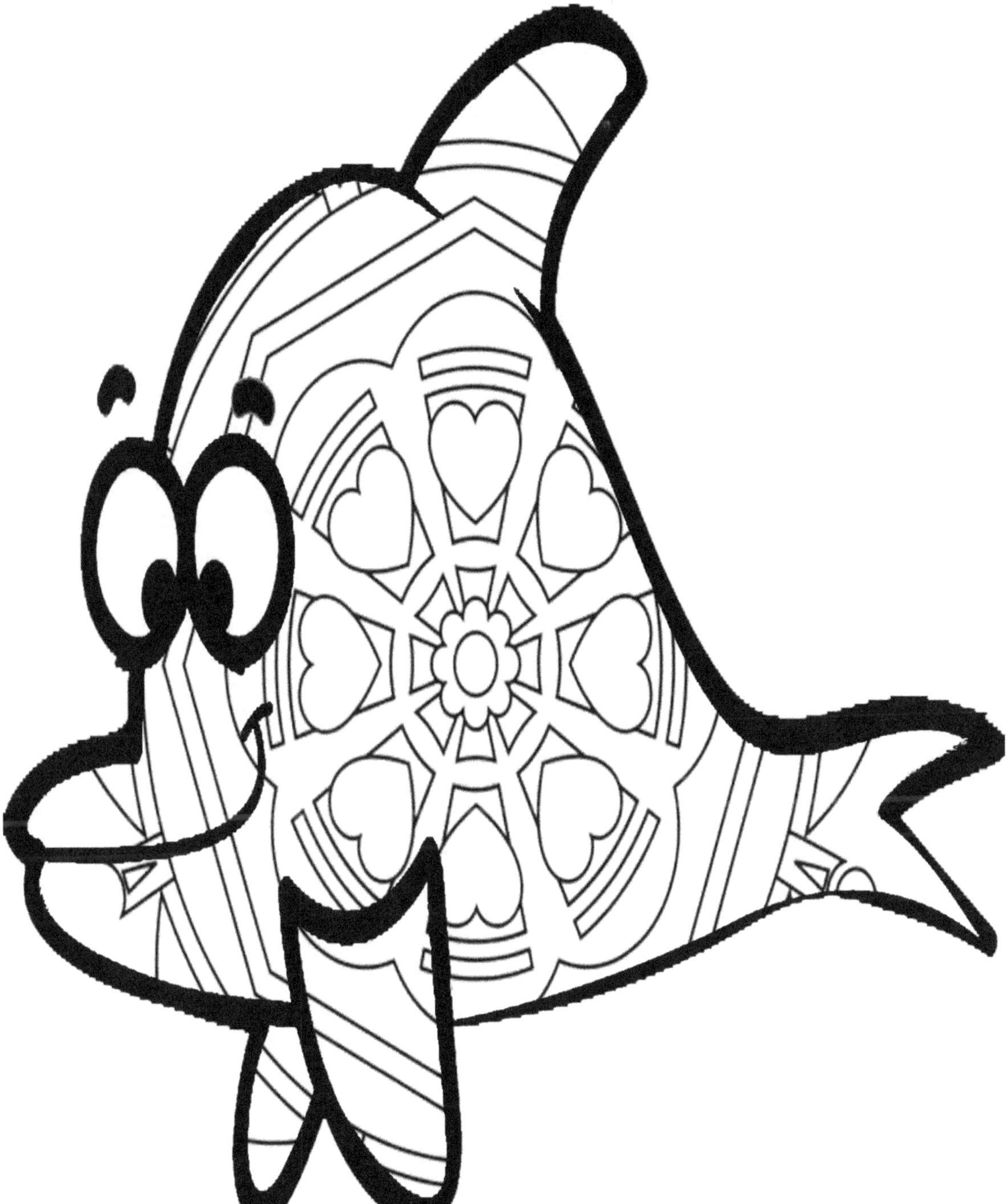

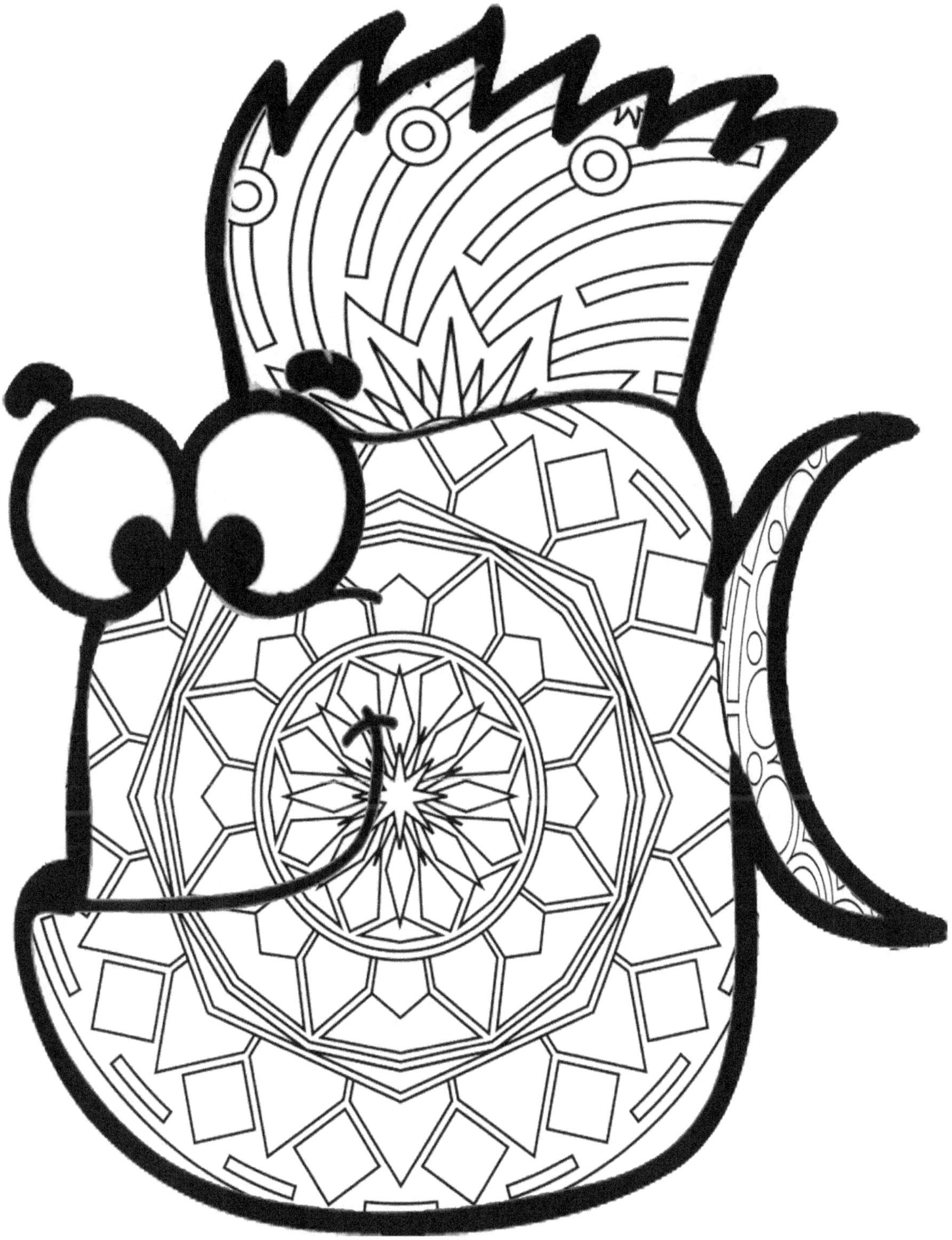

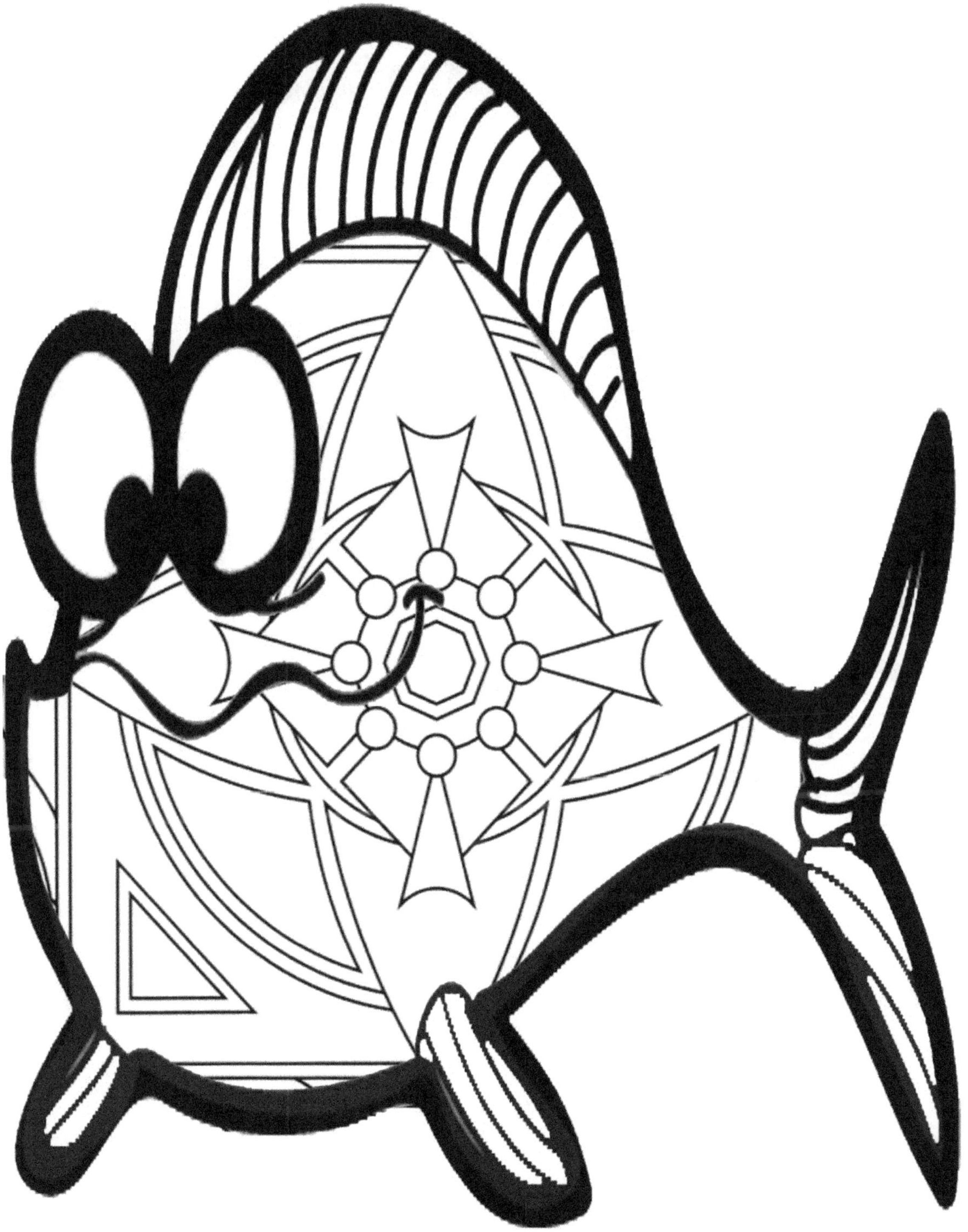

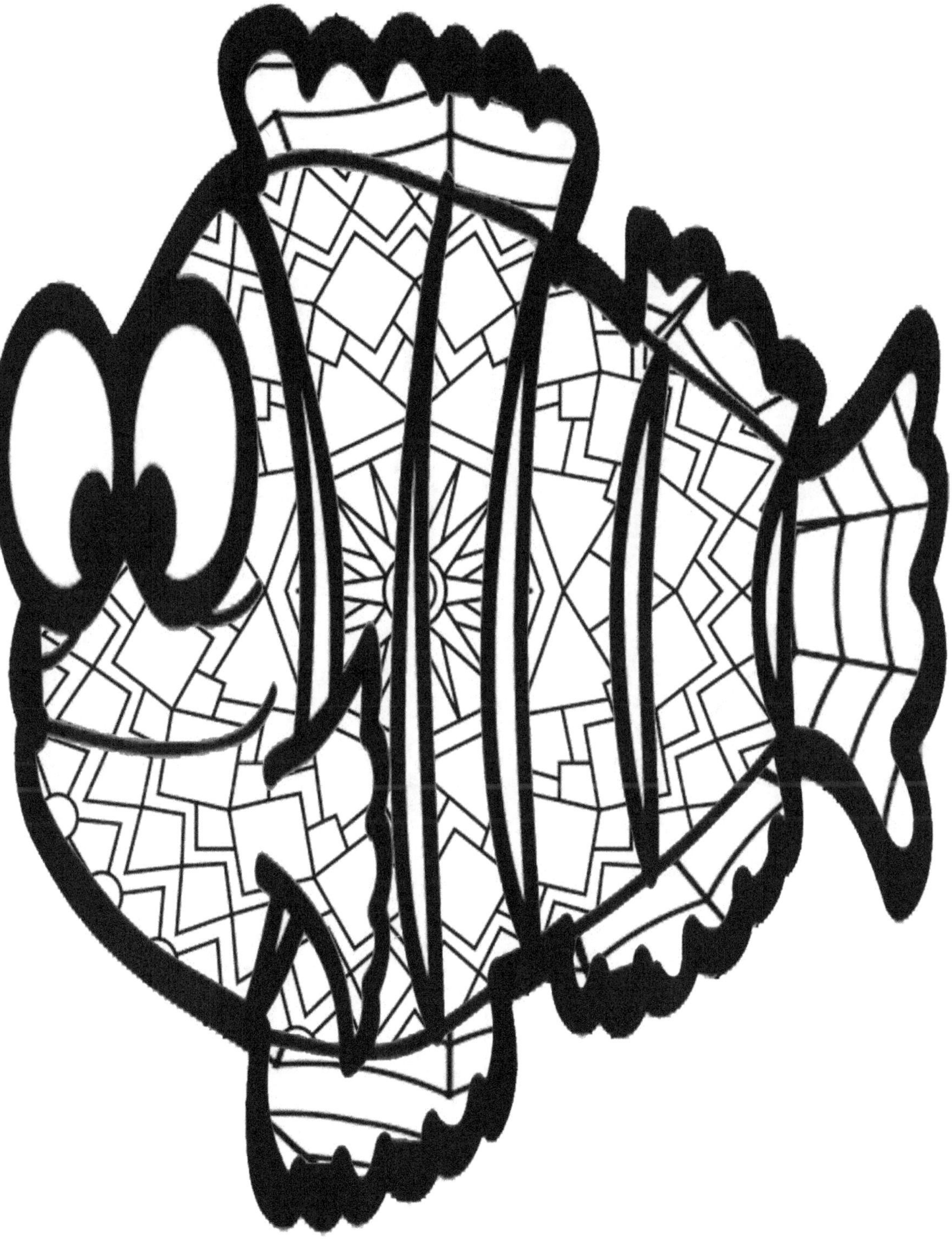

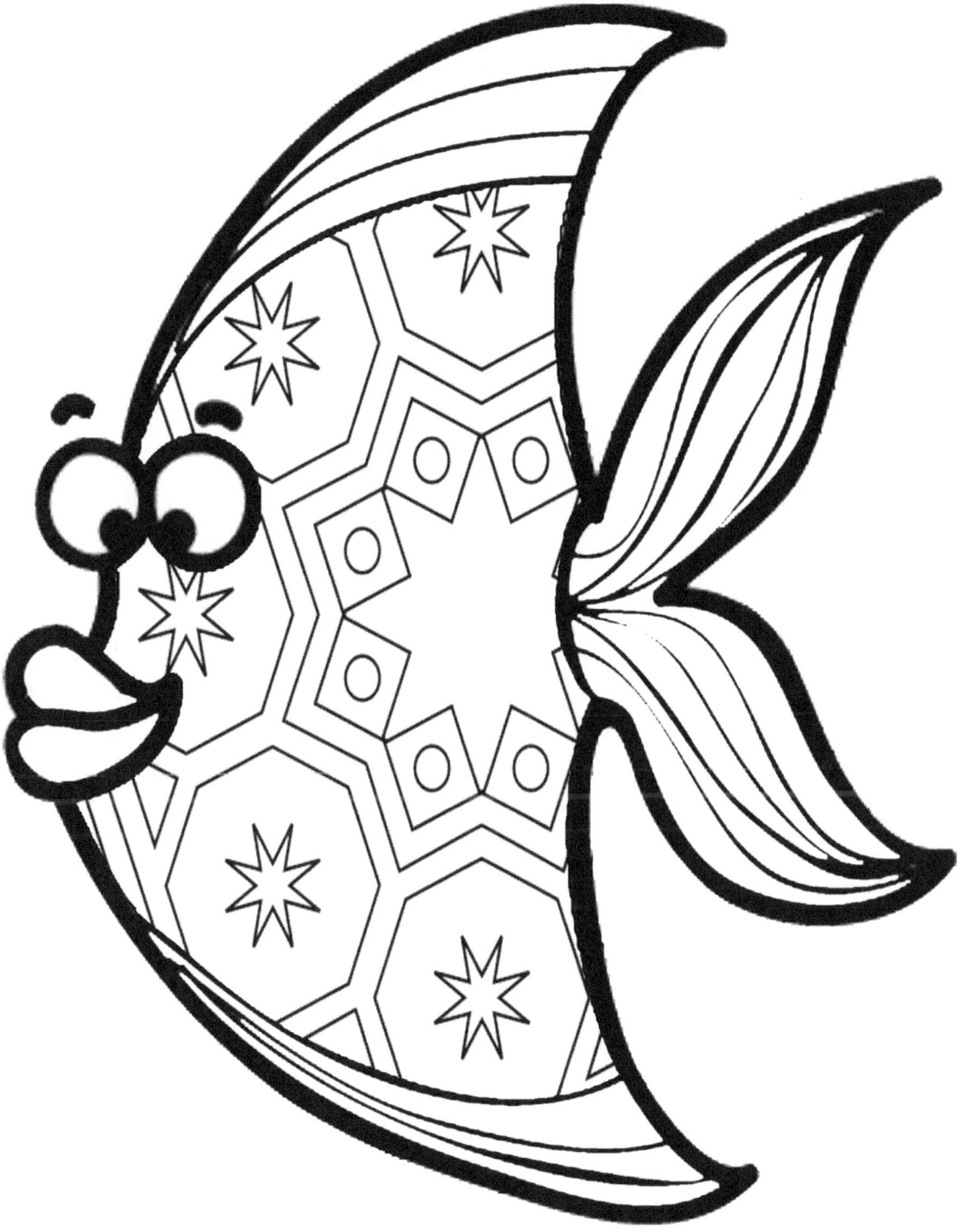

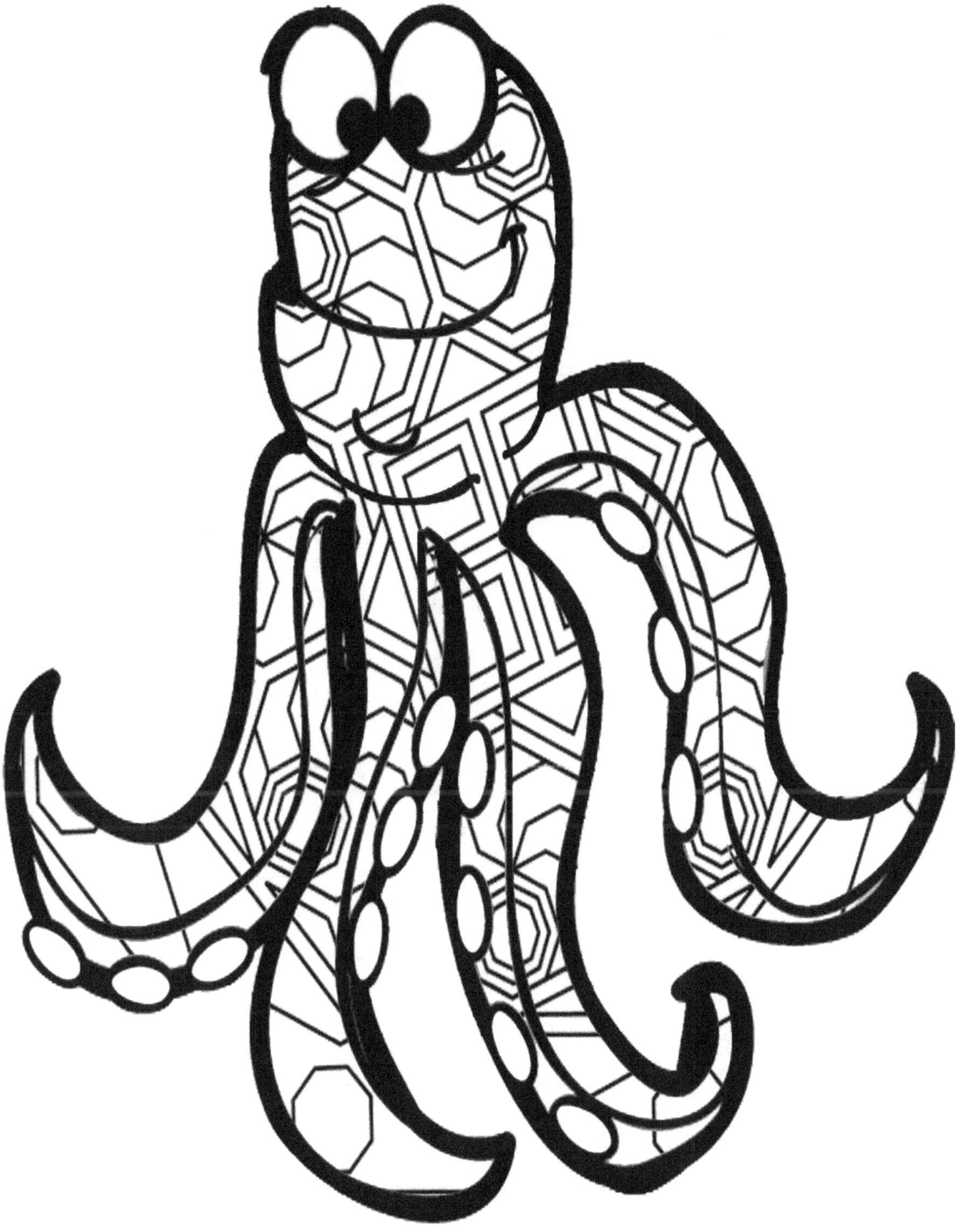

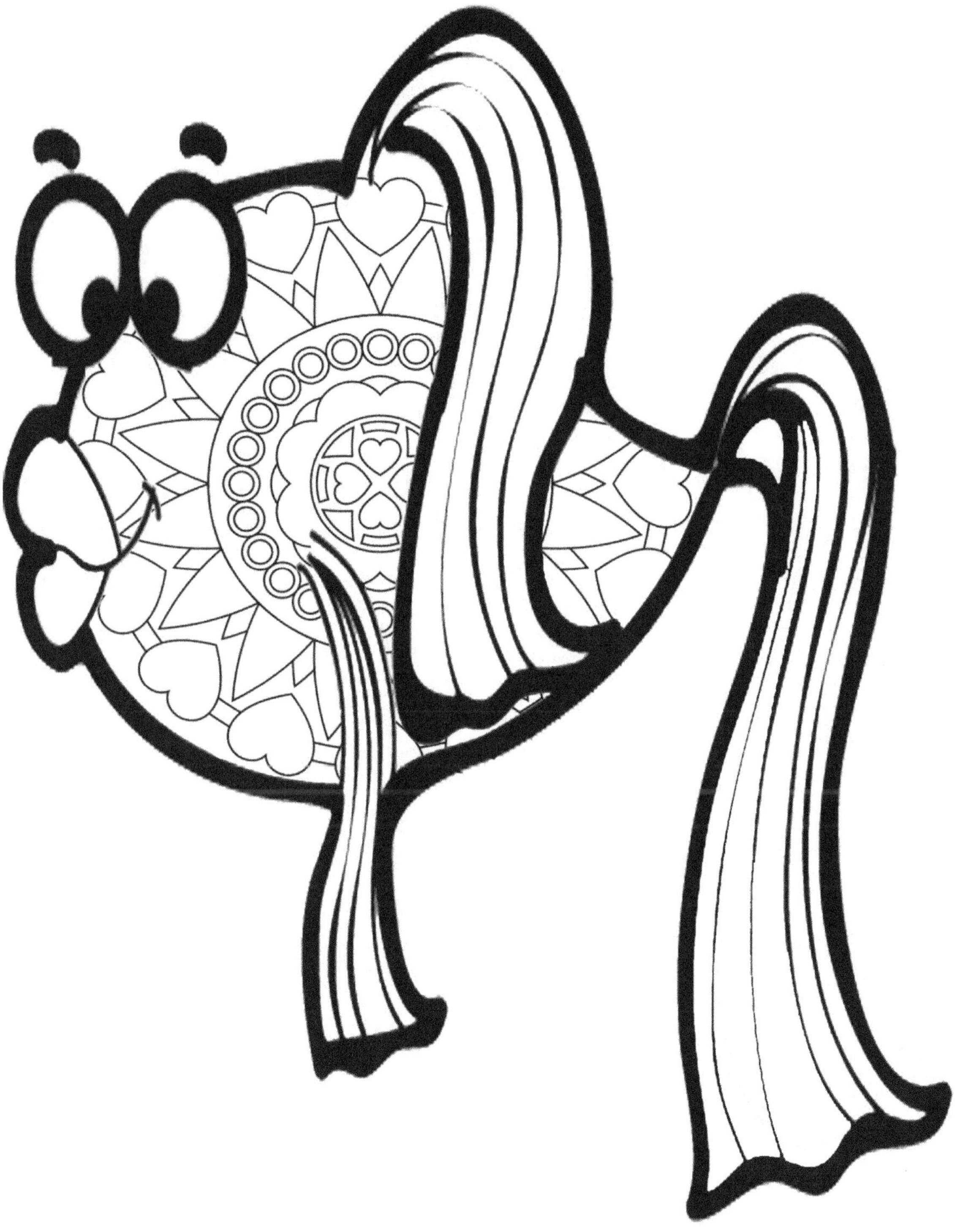

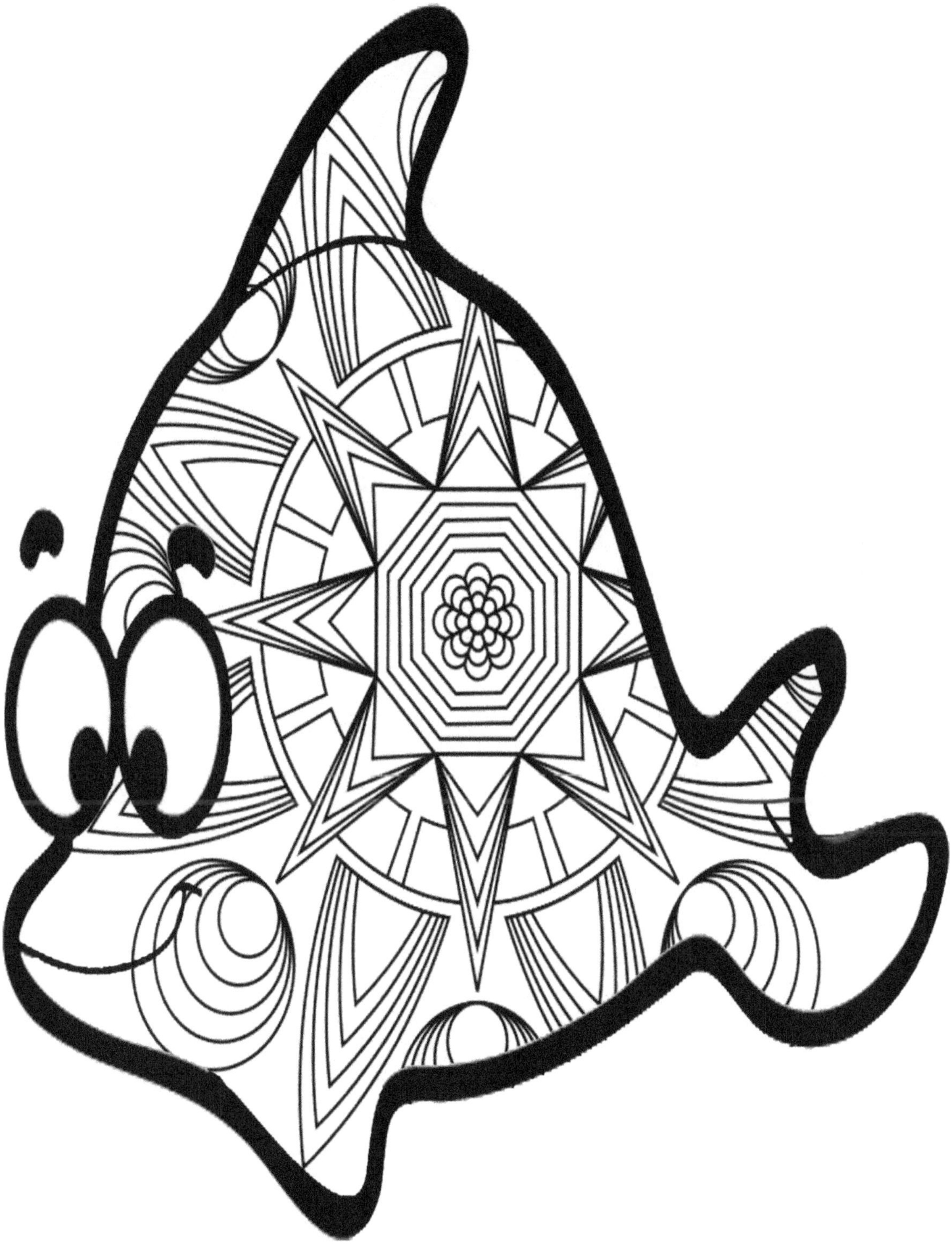

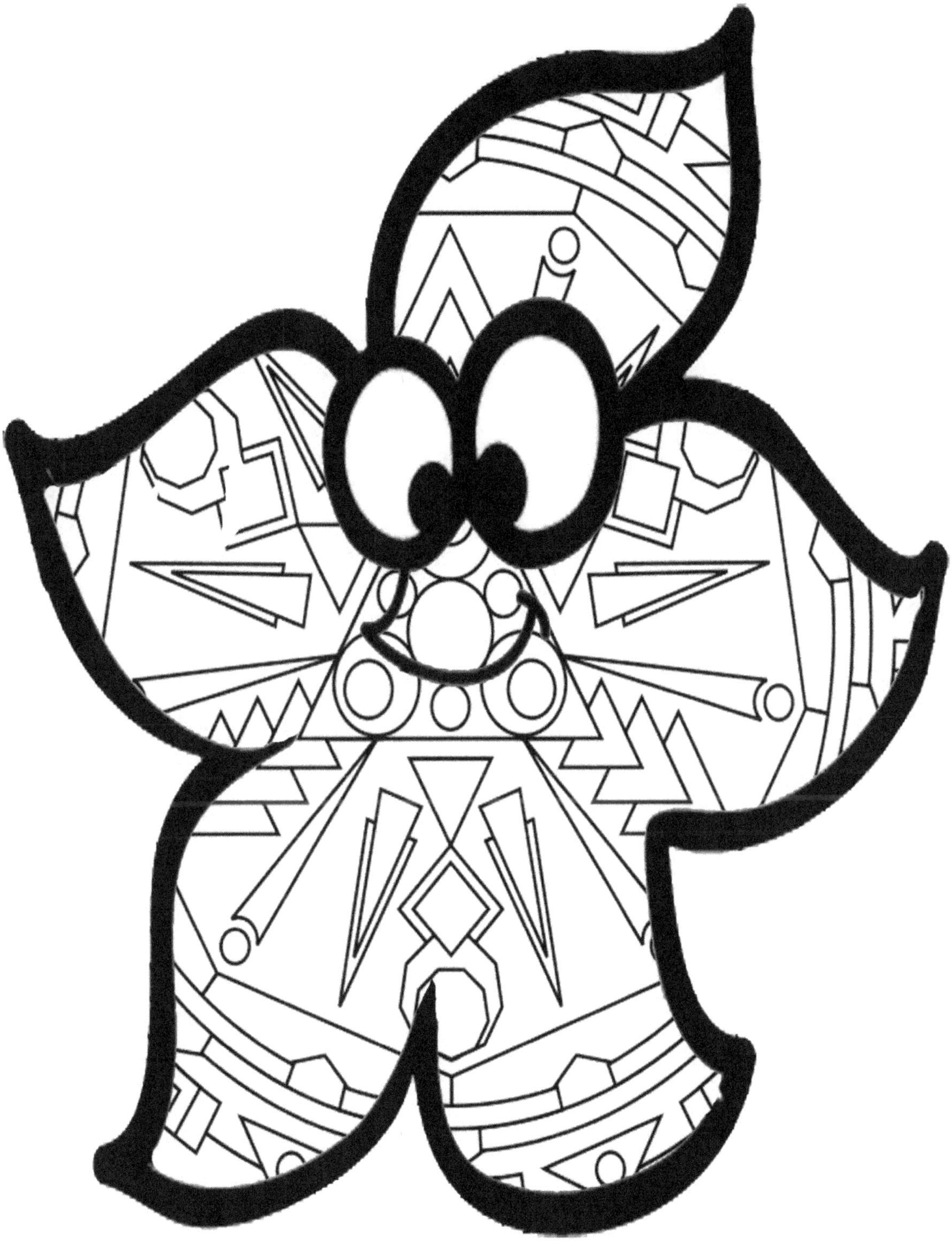

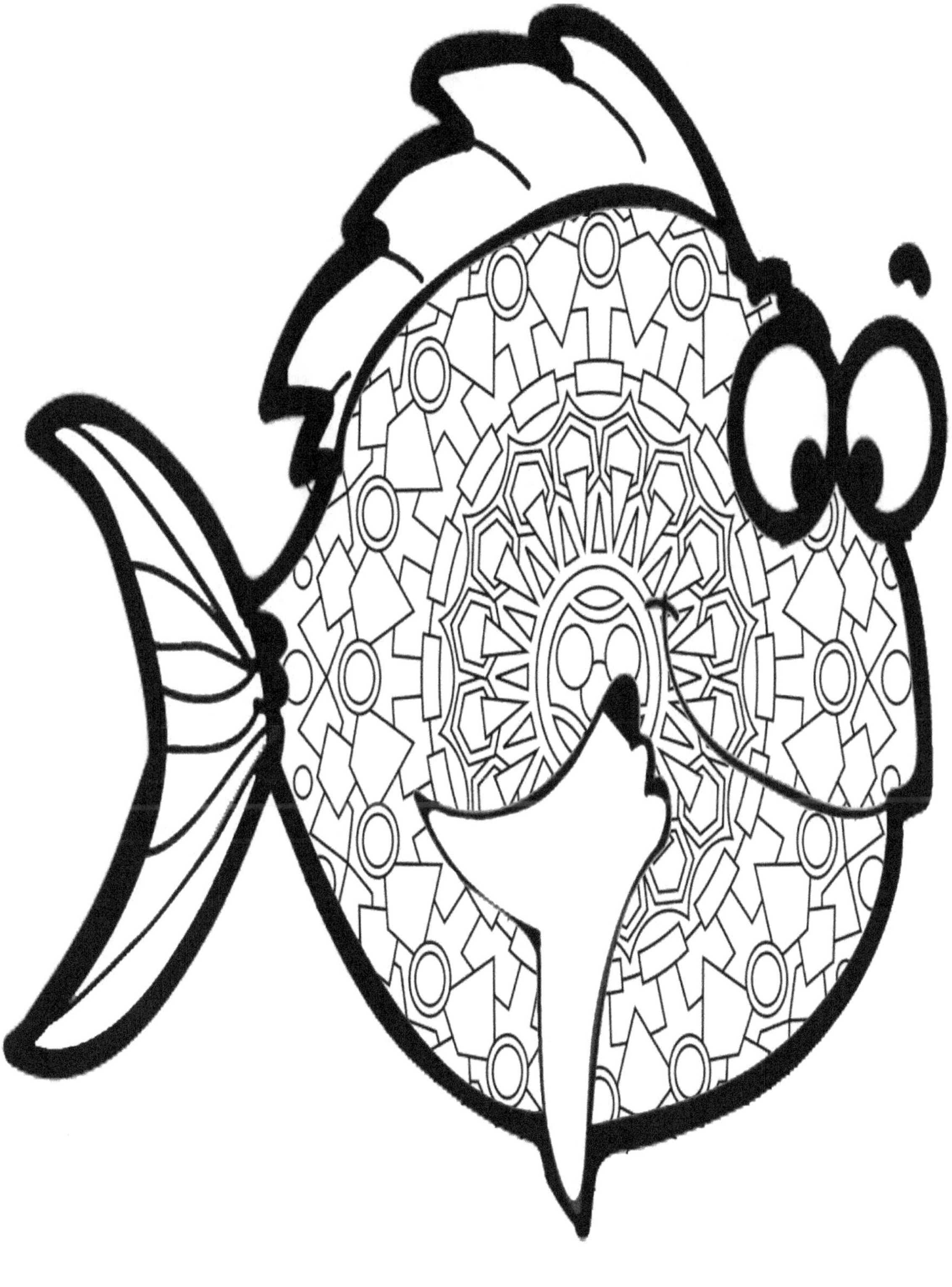

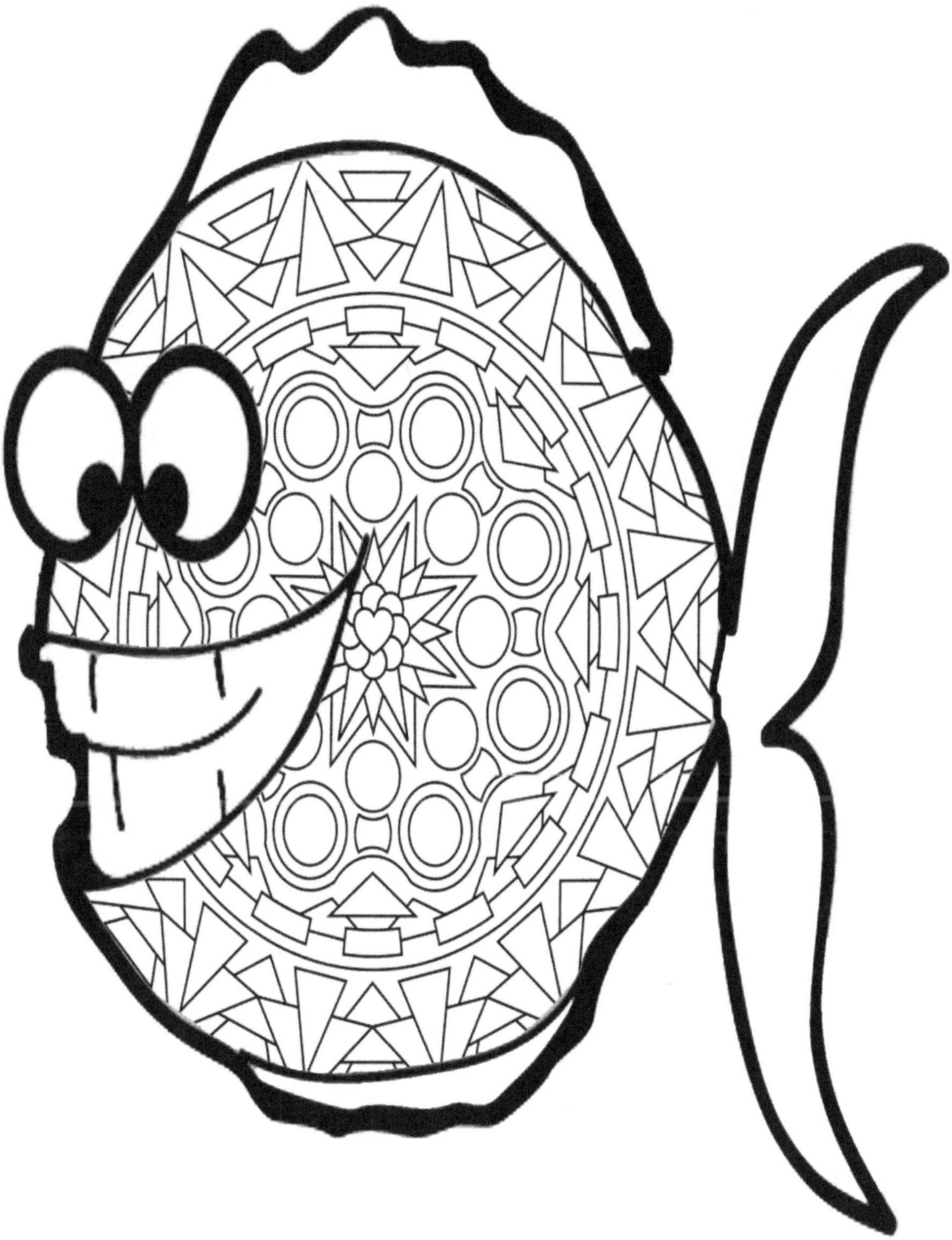

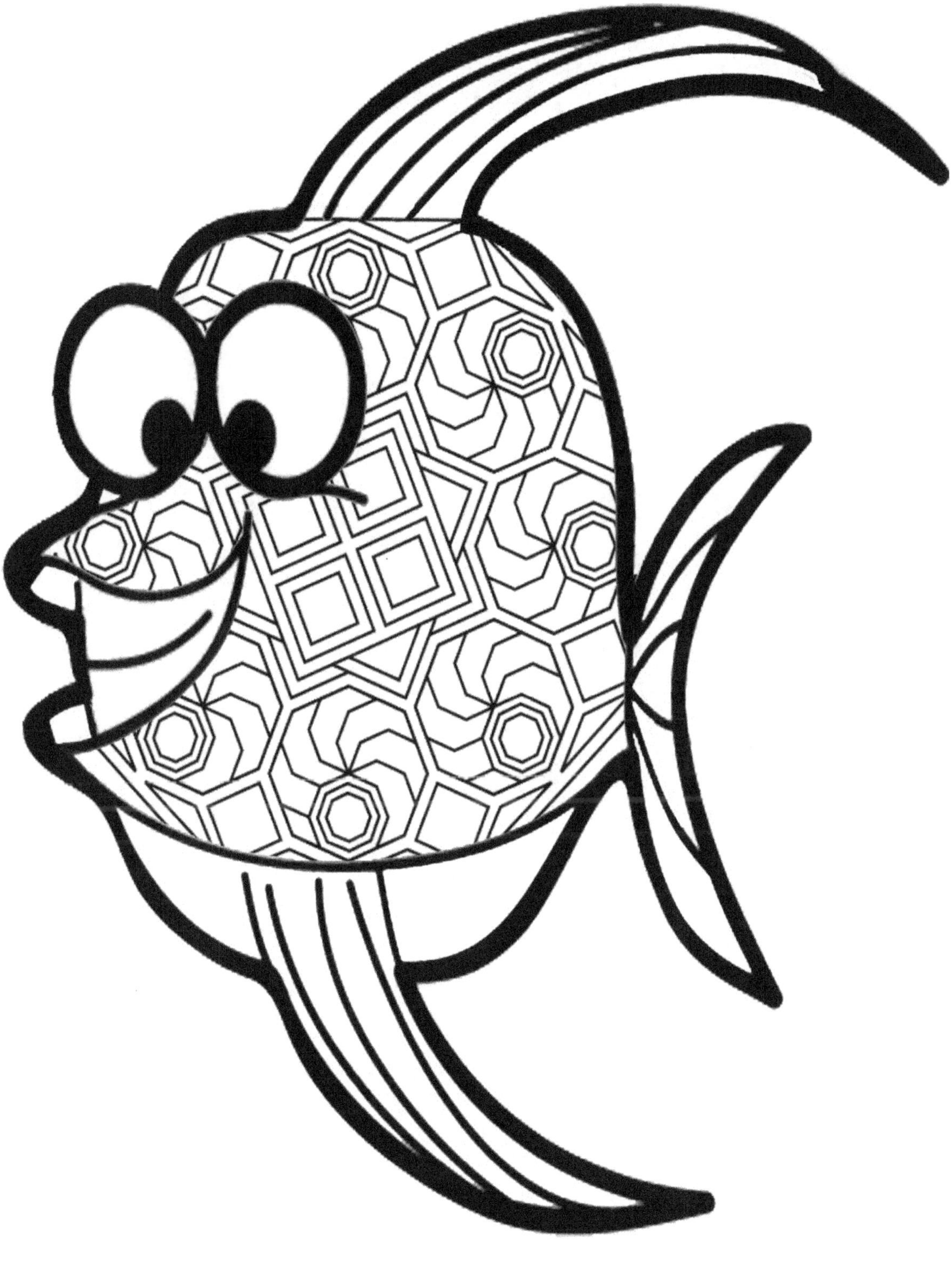

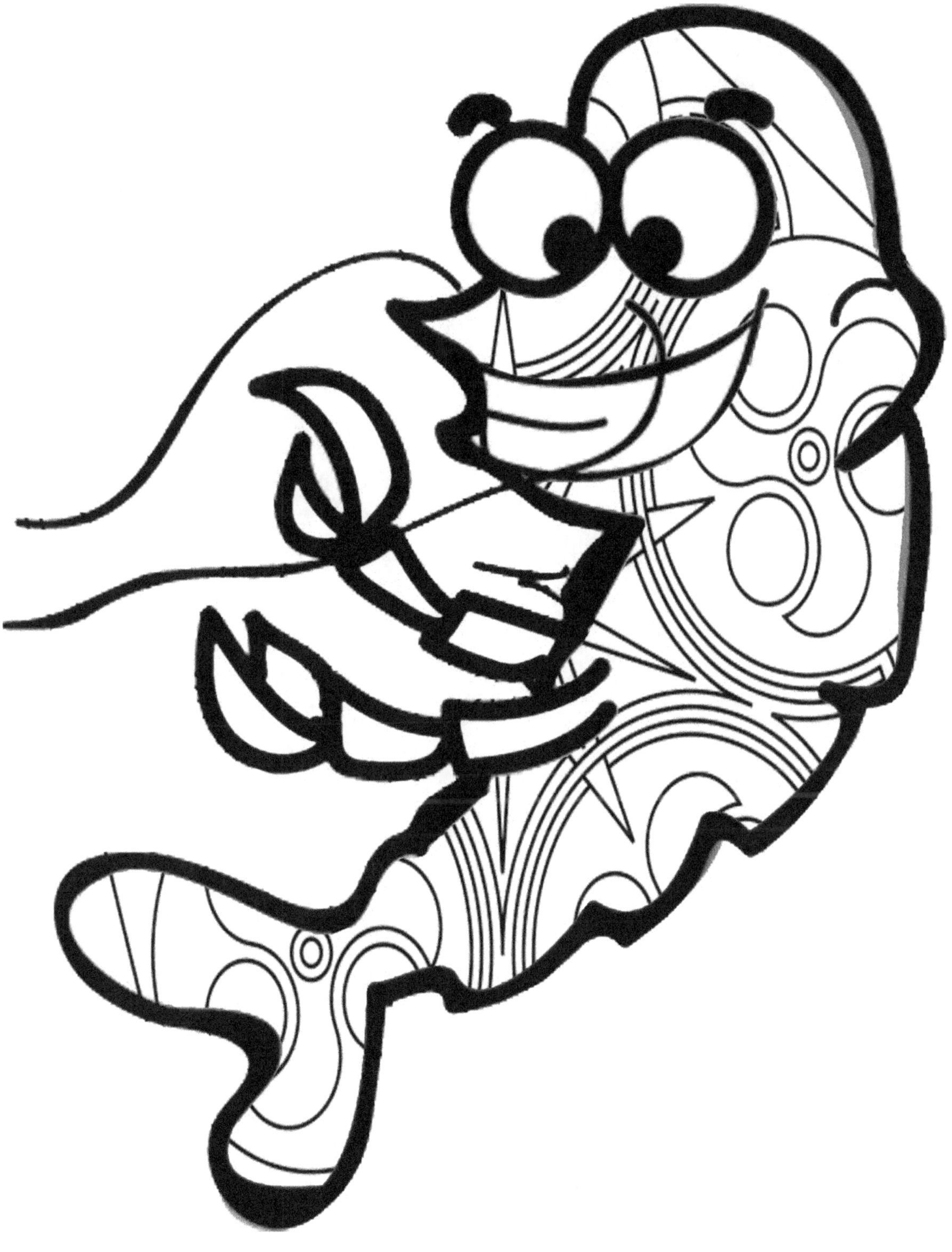

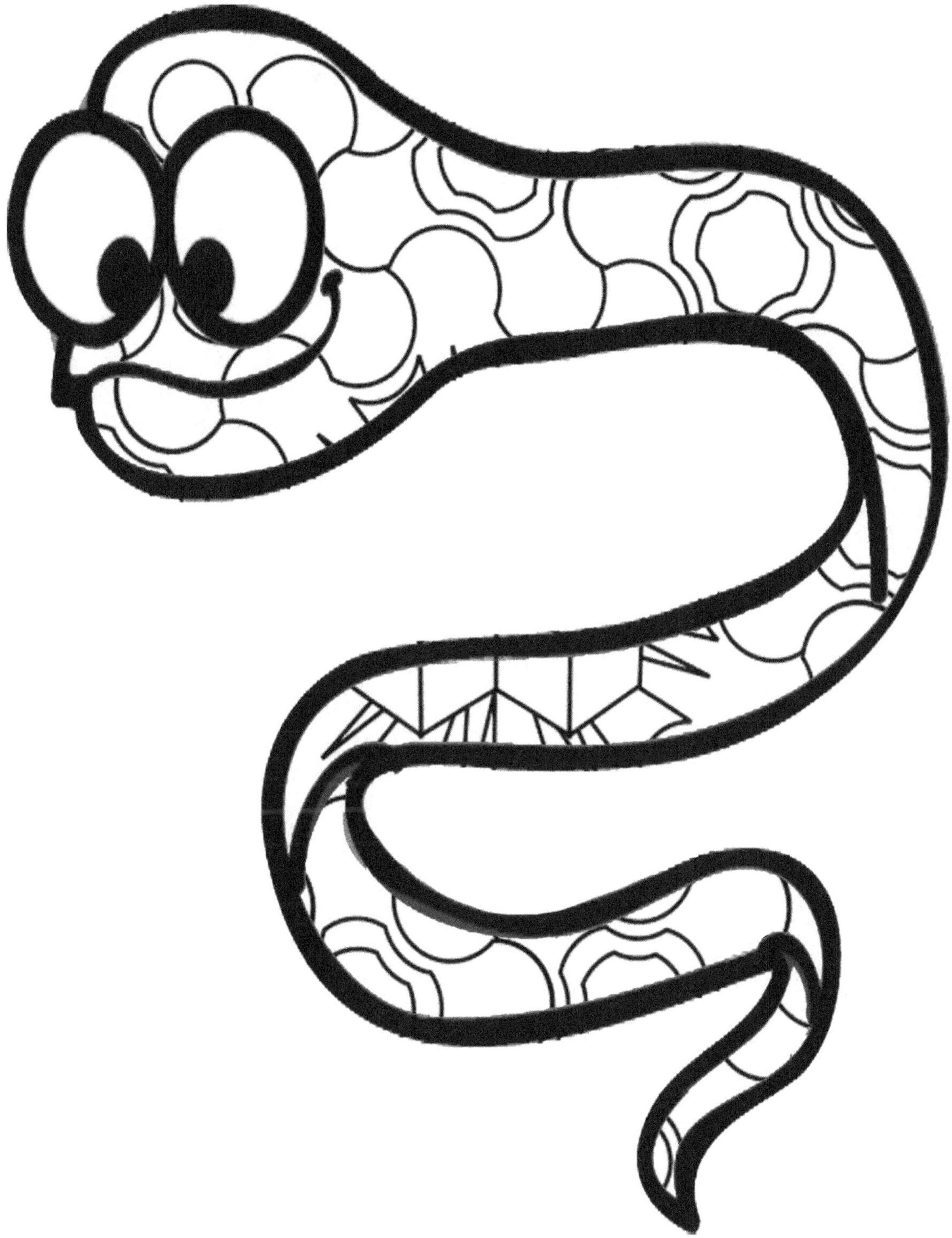

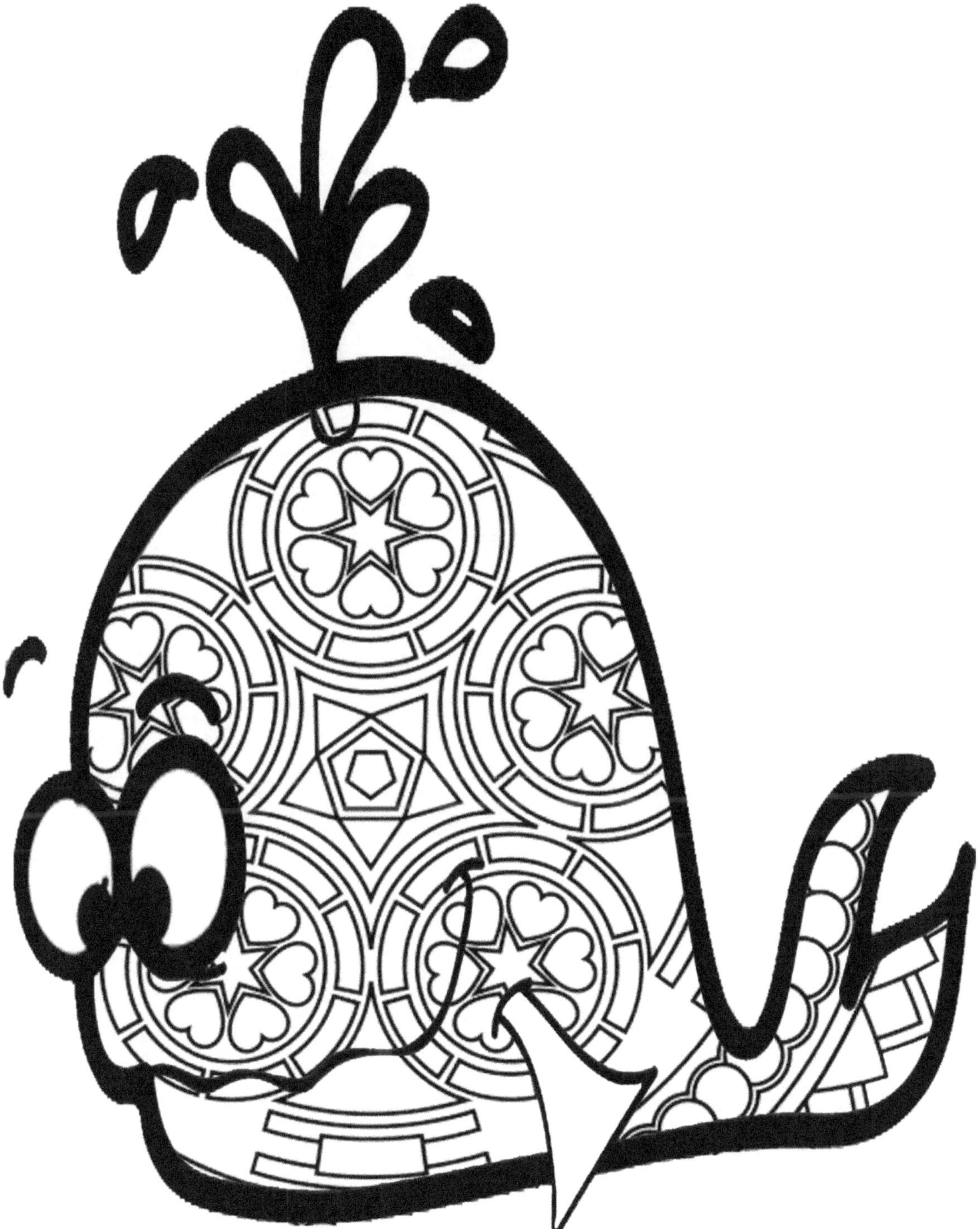

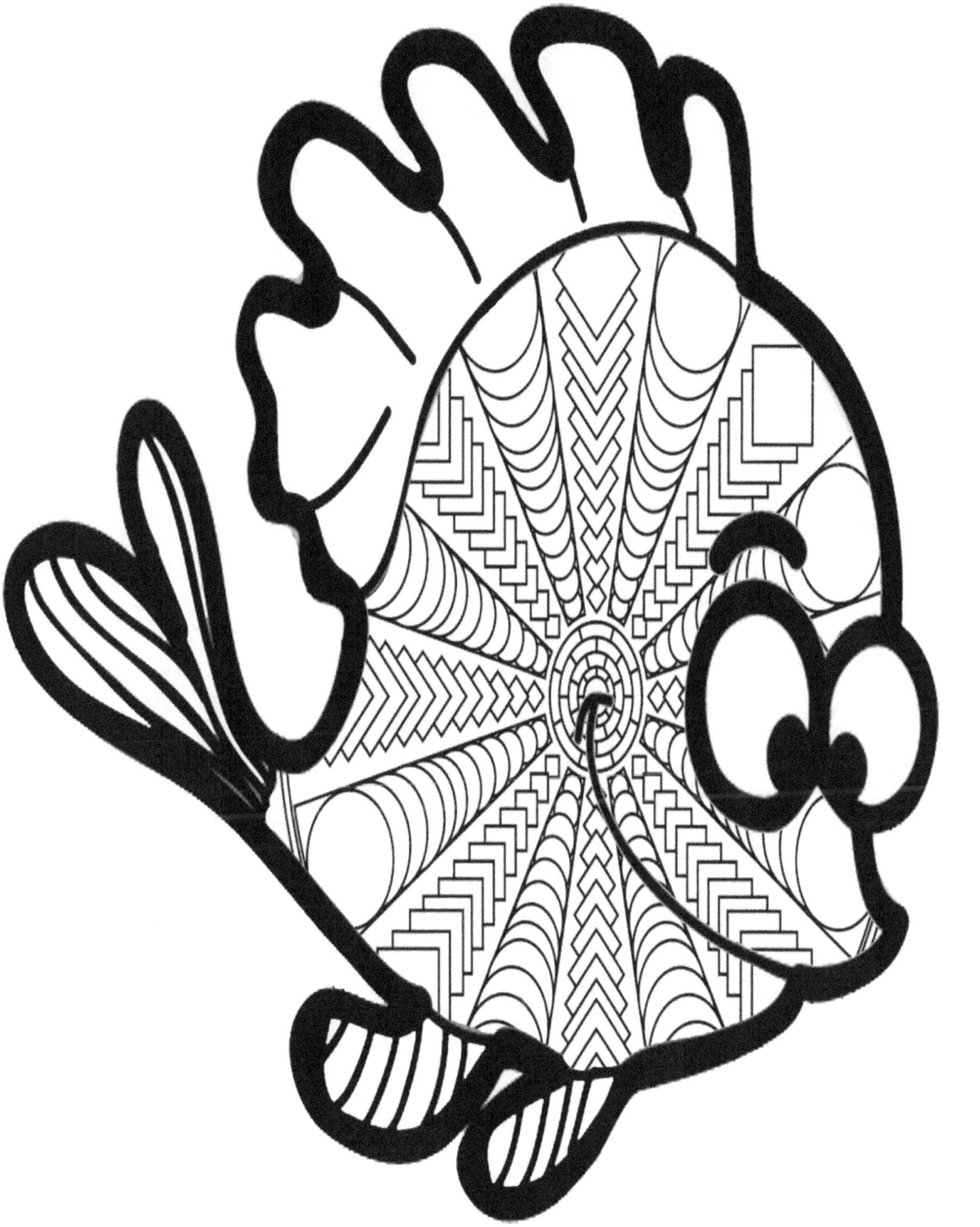

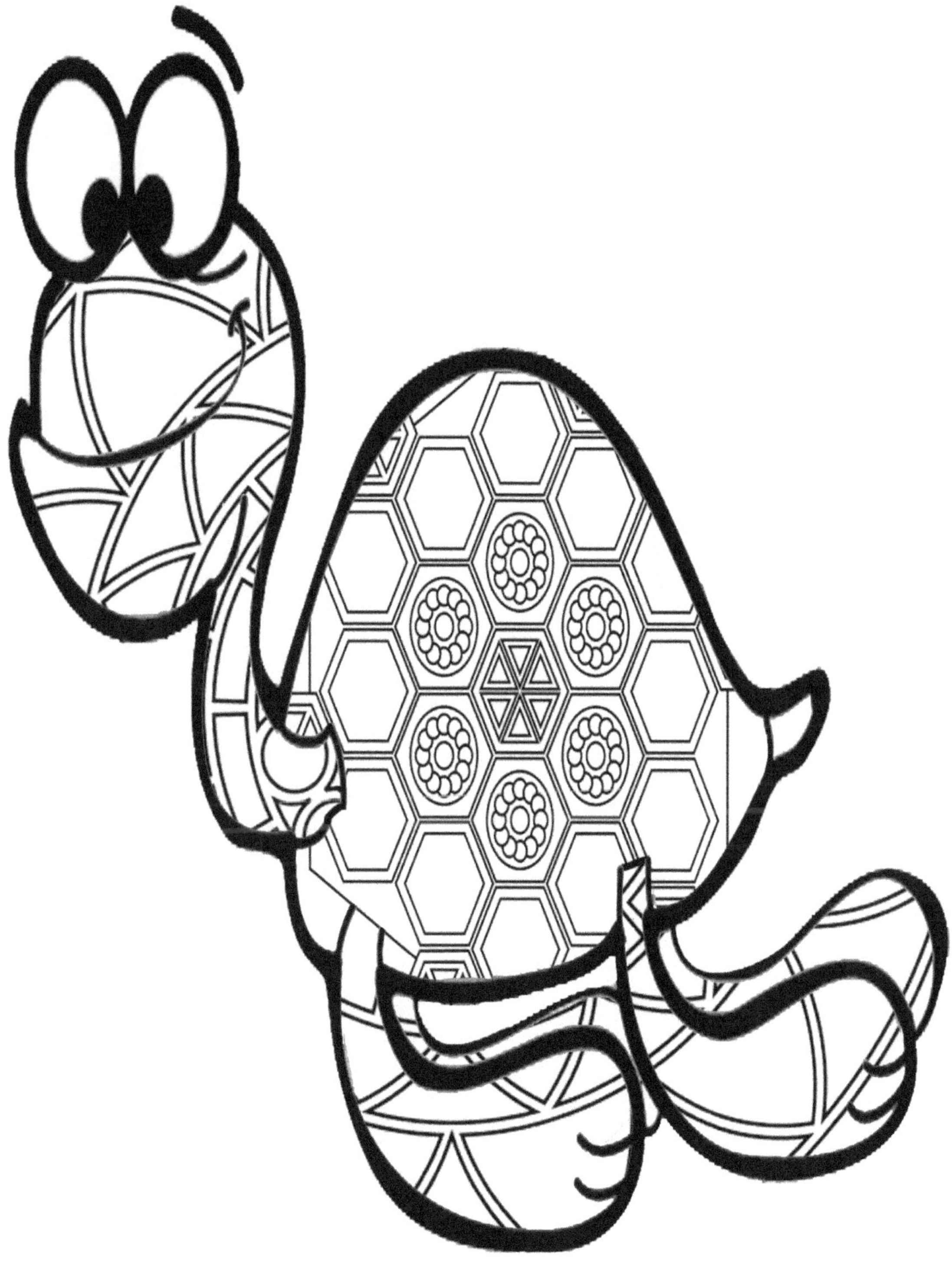

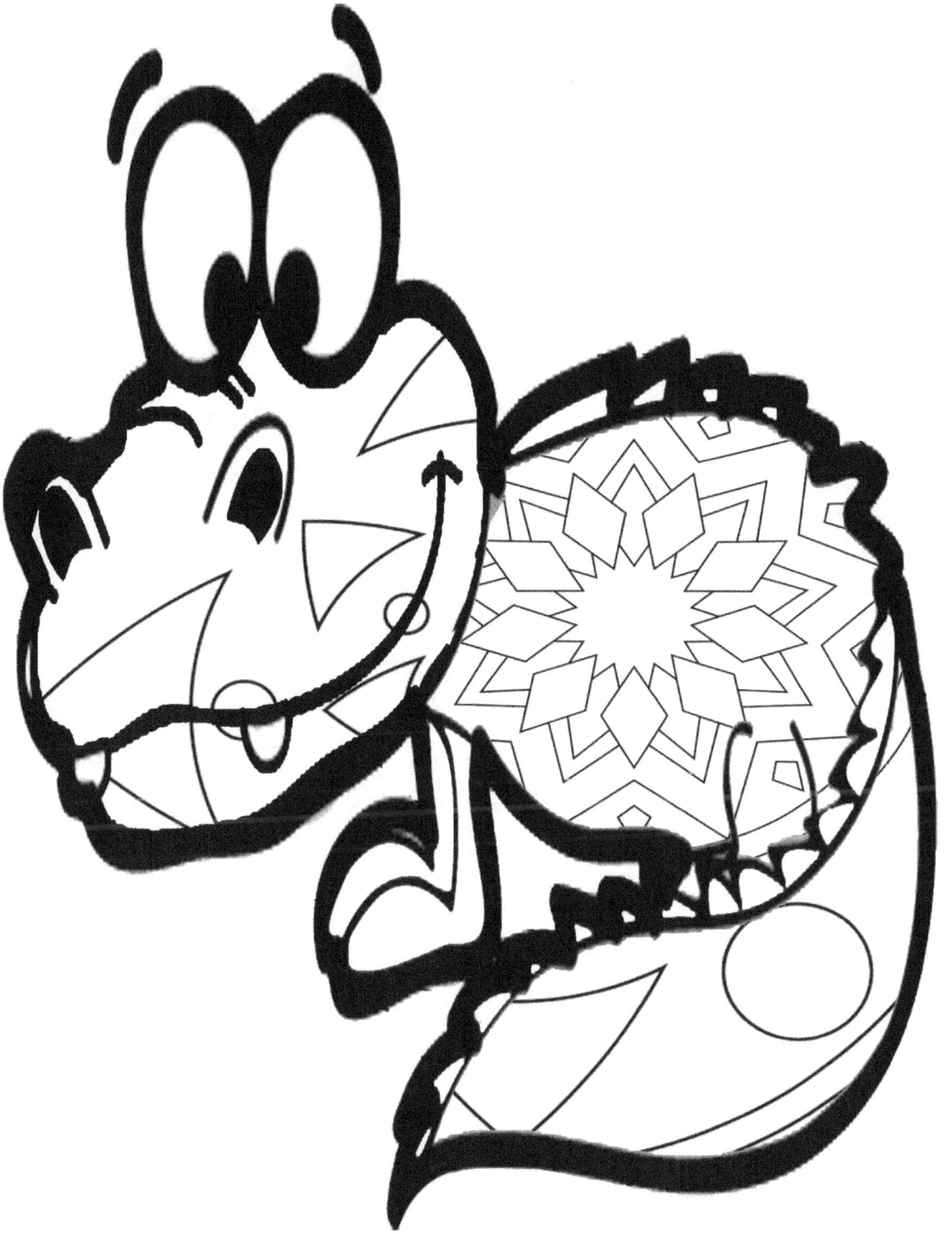

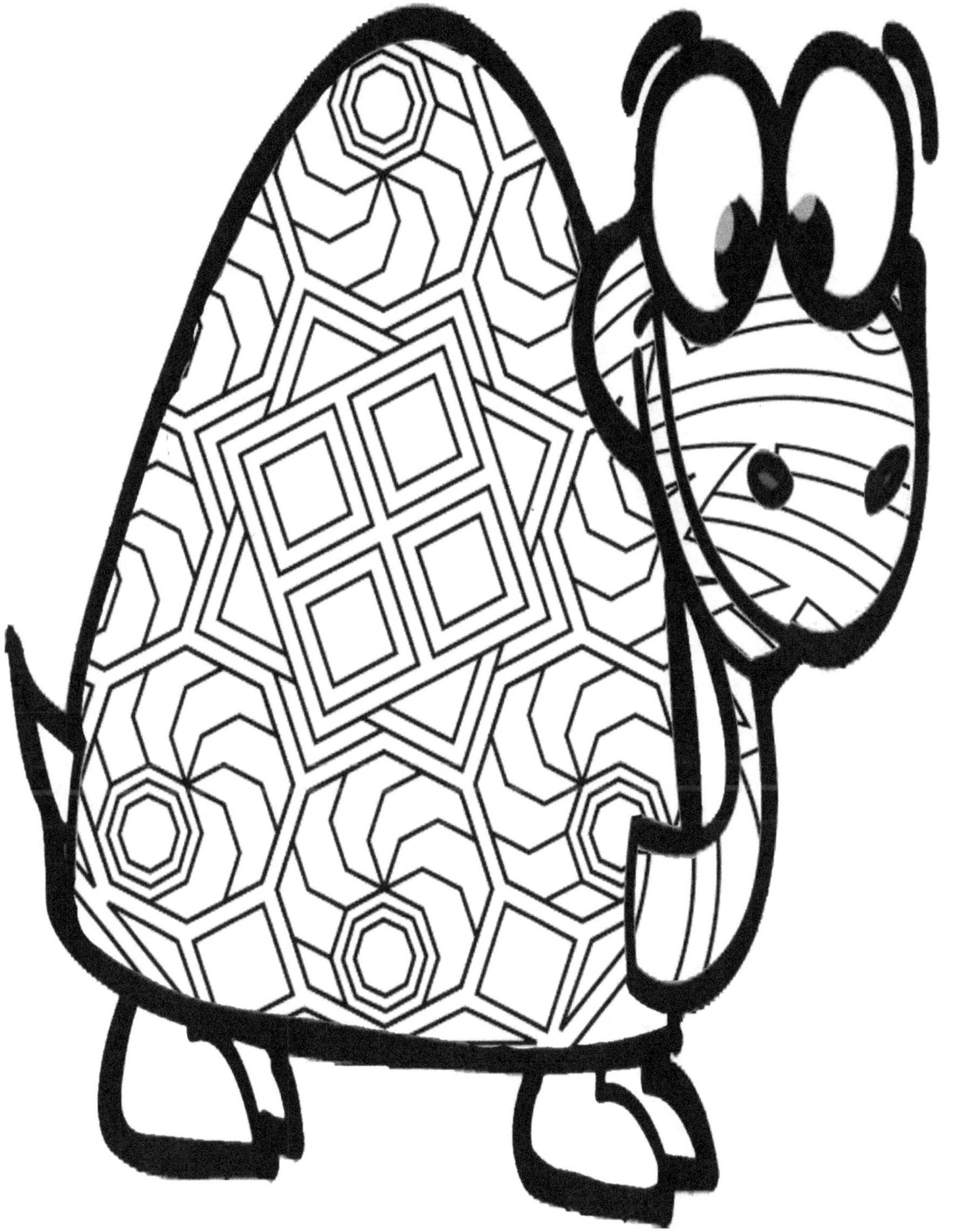

Thanks for coloring!

Helen B. Noble

www.ingramcontent.com/pod-product-compliance
Lightning Source LLC
Chambersburg PA
CBHW080608180526
45168CB00007B/2831